Follow The
FOOD
CHAIN

Who Ate the Frog?

A POND FOOD CHAIN

Sarah Ridley

Crabtree Publishing Company

www.crabtreebooks.com

D1194839

CRABTREE
PUBLISHING COMPANY
WWW.CRABTREEBOOKS.COM

Author: Sarah Ridley

Editorial director: Kathy Middleton

Editors: Nicola Edwards, Ellen Rodger

Proofreader: Crystal Sikkens

Designer: Lisa Peacock

Prepress technician: Samara Parent

Print coordinator: Katherine Berti

Photo credits:
FLPA: Konrad Wothe/Minden Pictures 11c.
iStock: MikeLane45 14t.
Nature PL: Alex Hyde 7, 12t; Willem Kolvoort 4; David Tipling 15t; Nick Upton 10t.
Shutterstock: Aloeks front cover tl; Bildagentur Zoonar GmbH front cover tr, 17br, 19br, 21cr; Gerry Bishop 15bc, 17bc, 19bc, 21br; Coulanges 6c; Ethan Daniels 4; Helen J Davies front cover bl, 11t; Morten Ekstroem 16t; Gail Johnson 18t; knelson20 19t; Malgorzata Ksiazkiewicz 2; Igor Krasilov 10br, 12br, 14br, 16br, 18br, 21cl; Lebendkulturen.de 6bc, 8bc, 10bc, 12bc, 14bc, 16bc, 18bc, 20bl; M-Foto 1; Milena 8bcr, 9, 10bcr, 12bcr, 14bcr, 16bcr, 18bcr, 20br; Chris Moody 22tr; Ondrej Prosicky 17t; Sue Robinson 13c; Rusya007 22b; Jordan Sharp 13bl, 15bl, 17bl, 19bl, 21bl; Nattawit Sronrachrudee 6bl, 8bl, 10bl, 12bl, 14bl, 16bl, 18bl, 20cl; sruilk 20-21bg; Rostislav Stefanek 8t; Trixcis 23tr; Rudmer Zwerver front cover br.

Every attempt has been made to clear copyright. Should there be any inadvertent omission please apply to the publisher for rectification.

Library and Archives Canada Cataloguing in Publication

Title: Who ate the frog? : a pond food chain / Sarah Ridley.
Names: Ridley, Sarah, 1963- author.
Description: Series statement: Follow the food chain |
  Previously published: London: Wayland, 2019. | Includes index.
Identifiers: Canadiana (print) 20190194960 |
  Canadiana (ebook) 20190194979 |
  ISBN 9780778771296 (hardcover) |
  ISBN 9780778771456 (softcover) |
  ISBN 9781427124524 (HTML)
Subjects: LCSH: Pond ecology—Juvenile literature. |
  LCSH: Food chains (Ecology)—Juvenile literature.
Classification: LCC QH541.5.P63 R53 2020 | DDC j577.63/6—dc23

Library of Congress Cataloging-in-Publication Data

Names: Ridley, Sarah, 1963- author.
Title: Who ate the frog? : a pond food chain / Sarah Ridley.
Description: New York : Crabtree Publishing Company, 2020. |
  Series: Follow the food chain | Includes index.
Identifiers: LCCN 2019043898 (print) | LCCN 2019043899 (ebook) |
  ISBN 9780778771296 (hardcover) |
  ISBN 9780778771456 (paperback) |
  ISBN 9781427124524 (ebook)
Subjects: LCSH: Food chains (Ecology)--Juvenile literature. |
  Pond ecology--Juvenile literature.
Classification: LCC QH541.15.F66 R535 2020 (print) | LCC QH541.15.
  F66 (ebook) | DDC 577.63/6--dc23
LC record available at https://lccn.loc.gov/2019043898
LC ebook record available at https://lccn.loc.gov/2019043899

Crabtree Publishing Company

www.crabtreebooks.com   1–800–387–7650

Published by Crabtree Publishing Company in 2020

First published in Great Britain in 2019 by Wayland
Copyright ©Hodder and Stoughton, 2019

Printed in the U.S.A./012020/CG20191115

Published in Canada
Crabtree Publishing
616 Welland Ave.
St. Catharines, Ontario
L2M 5V6

Published in the United States
Crabtree Publishing
PMB 59051
350 Fifth Avenue, 59th Floor
New York, New York 10118

CONTENTS

Food for life

All living things need food to give them the **energy** to live. Plants make their own food using energy from sunlight, air, soil, and water.

The leaves of water lilies float on the surface of ponds. They capture sunlight to make food for the plants to grow.

Animals cannot make their own food. They eat plants or other animals to survive. This **tadpole** is eating algae. Algae are living things that make their own food. In turn, many animals eat tadpoles.

Algae live in ponds, lakes, rivers, and oceans.

Plants and animals are linked together by many different **food chains**. This book looks at a pond food chain.

Who eats what and where?

Many different plants and types of algae live underwater. They soak up the rays of sunlight that pass through the water. Others float on the surface or grow on the edge of ponds.

← Fish find shelter among underwater plants.

↓ Everything that lives, needs energy to grow. This food chain shows the food energy moving from one living thing to another.

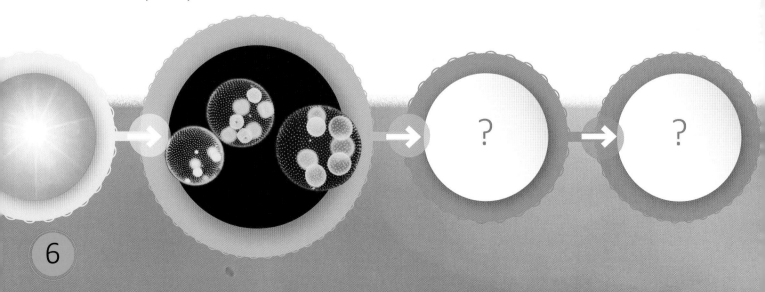

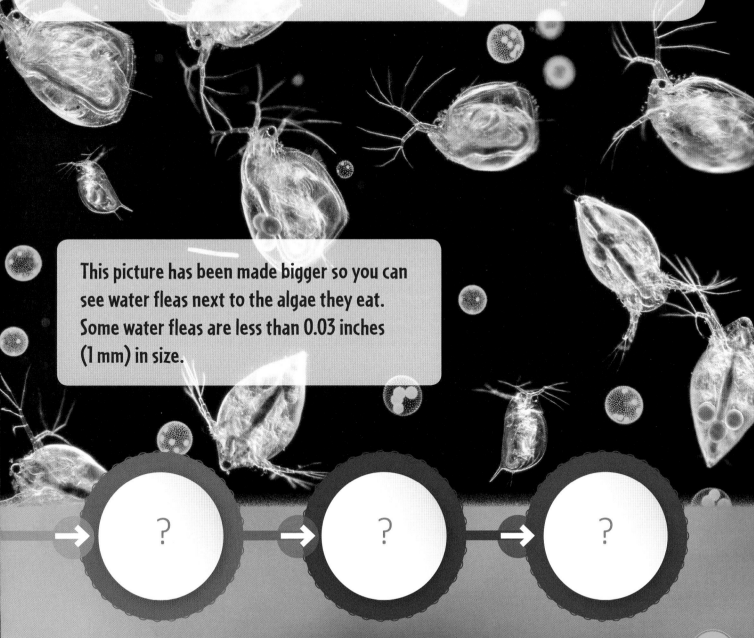

Algae come in all shapes and sizes. Some look like plants. Others are so small we need a **microscope** to see them. They all make their own food using sunlight, like plants do. Unlike plants, they do not have roots or leaves.

This picture has been made bigger so you can see water fleas next to the algae they eat. Some water fleas are less than 0.03 inches (1 mm) in size.

Who ate the algae?

A mayfly **larva** ate the algae! A mayfly can spend up to two years crawling around the bottom of the pond. Then it is ready to turn into an adult mayfly.

Mayfly larvae eat algae and tiny bits of rotting plants. Dragonfly and damselfly larvae eat animals, including mayfly larvae!

When it is ready to change into an adult, the larva floats to the surface of the pond. It then sheds its skin and flies out of the water. Once it has dried out, it sheds its skin again. It is now an adult.

Mayflies usually live for less than a day. This is just long enough to mate and lay eggs.

Who ate the mayfly?

A damselfly ate the mayfly. It caught the mayfly in midair and flew to a plant leaf to eat it.

This damselfly is eating a mayfly.

Damselflies and dragonflies look almost the same. One way to tell them apart is a damselfly rests with its wings folded together. A dragonfly stretches its wings out.

Dragonfly

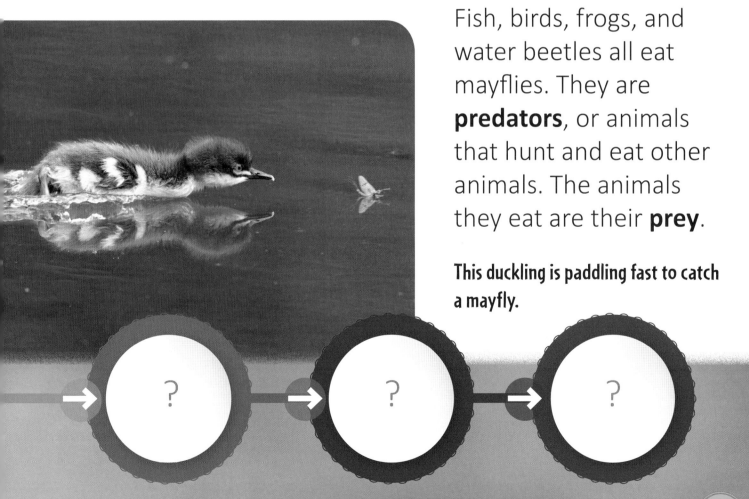

Fish, birds, frogs, and water beetles all eat mayflies. They are **predators**, or animals that hunt and eat other animals. The animals they eat are their **prey**.

This duckling is paddling fast to catch a mayfly.

→ ?　→ ?　→ ?

Who ate the damselfly?

A raft spider ate the damselfly. Can you spot a wing floating on the water?

The hairs on the spider's legs help it to float as it moves across the surface of the pond.

When the damselfly dipped into the water to cool off, the spider's legs felt the movement across the water's surface. The spider left its hiding place at the edge of the pond, and rushed out to grab the damselfly.

Raft spiders mostly eat pond skaters, dragonfly larvae, and small spiders.

Pond skater

Who ate the raft spider?

A frog ate the raft spider. It flicked out its long, sticky tongue to catch the spider before it ran away. Frogs also eat dragonflies, flies, slugs, snails, and worms.

A frog's large eyes spot movement. This helps it hunt for food, and escape danger.

Frogs lay eggs called frog spawn, in ponds. Tadpoles hatch from the eggs. They grow into froglets and then become frogs.

The black dots in the frog spawn will hatch into tadpoles.

?

15

Who ate the frog?

A heron waited and watched. It grabbed the frog and gobbled it up.

A heron's long legs let it wade into water in search of food.

Herons mostly eat fish, as well as voles, newts, and ducklings. Look for herons by rivers, lakes, and ponds.

This heron will swallow a fish whole, without chewing. It has no teeth.

Who ate the heron?

No one ate the heron. Herons are big birds. It is unlikely that another animal will catch them. They are the top predator in a pond.

Herons have huge wings that help them fly away from danger.

In some areas of the world, herons **migrate** in fall. It is too cold for them to find food in winter. They return in spring to mate and have babies.

Follow who eats what

Energy from the Sun is made into food by plants and algae. Animals then eat plants, algae, or other animals.

Can you remember the links in the pond food chain shown in this book? The answers are shown below.

1. Sunlight 2. Algae 3. Mayfly and larva 4. Damselfly 5. Raft spider 6. Frog 7. Heron

Pond links

What eats what in a pond depends on where in the world the pond is located. In North America, pond plants may include cattails and water lilies. Pond animals may include snapping turtles, beavers, catfish, and red-wing blackbirds.

Beaver

Ponds are threatened by **pollution**. Pollution includes all the things that get washed into ponds when it rains. Pollution can make a lot of algae grow over the surface of ponds (above). This threatens all life in and around the pond.

Useful words

energy The ability to move and do work. Food energy keeps a living thing alive and allows it to move, breathe, or work in some other way.

food chain The plants and animals linked together by what eats what

larva A young insect

mate To come together to make babies

microscope A device that uses lenses to make very small things appear larger

migrate To move from one place to another, usually in spring and fall, for feeding or breeding

pollution Damage caused to water, air, or wild areas by harmful substances such as chemicals, litter, or human waste

pond A small area of fresh, still water

predator An animal that hunts and eats other animals

prey An animal that is hunted and killed by another animal for food

tadpole A young frog, toad, or newt

Index